The · Life Cycle · Series

The Life Cycle of a
Lion

Bobbie Kalman & Amanda Bishop

Crabtree Publishing Company

www.crabtreebooks.com

The Life Cycle Series
A Bobbie Kalman Book

Dedicated by Amanda Bishop
For Mummu and Grampsie, whose pride has always meant the world to me

Editor-in-Chief
Bobbie Kalman

Writing team
Bobbie Kalman
Amanda Bishop

Editors
Niki Walker
Kathryn Smithyman

Copy editor
Jaimie Nathan

Cover and title page design
Campbell Creative Services

Computer design
Margaret Amy Reiach

Production coordinator
Heather Fitzpatrick

Photo researcher
Jaimie Nathan

Consultant
Patricia Loesche, PhD., Animal Behavior Program,
Department of Psychology, University of Washington

Photographs
Erwin and Peggy Bauer/Wildstock: page 6
Michael Turco: pages 16, 17
Other images by Corbis Images, Digital Stock,
and Digital Vision

Illustrations
Bonna Rouse: pages 5 (top right and bottom left),
6, 7 (bottom right), 9, 13, 14, 30
Barbara Bedell: pages 5 (bottom right), 7 (bottom left),
18, 26, 27, 29, 30, 31
Margaret Amy Reiach: series logo, page 17
Tiffany Wybouw: lion border, page 10

Digital prepress and printing
Worzalla Publishing Company

Crabtree Publishing Company

www.crabtreebooks.com   1-800-387-7650

PMB 16A
350 Fifth Avenue
Suite 3308
New York, NY
10118

612 Welland Avenue
St. Catharines
Ontario
Canada
L2M 5V6

73 Lime Walk
Headington
Oxford
OX3 7AD
United Kingdom

Cataloging-in-Publication Data
Kalman, Bobbie
  The life cycle of a lion / Bobbie Kalman & Amanda Bishop.
    p. cm. -- (The life cycle series)
Includes index.
Presents information about lions, including what constitutes a pride, how lion cubs are raised, hunting, competition, and some of the dangers lions face today.
  ISBN 0-7787-0686-9 (pbk.) -- ISBN 0-7787-0656-7 (RLB)
  1. Lions--Life cycles--Juvenile literature. [1. Lions.]
I. Bishop, Amanda. II. Title.
  QL737.C23 K348 2002
  599.757--dc21

                           LC 2002002276

Contents

What is a lion?

A lion is a **mammal**. A mammal is a **warm-blooded** animal. Its body stays at about the same temperature even when the temperature of its surroundings changes. A baby mammal is born with hair or fur and drinks milk from its mother's body.

Cat family members

Lions are members of the cat family, *Felidae*. They are close relatives of large roaring cats such as tigers and leopards. Lions are **carnivores**, or meat-eaters. They are **predators** that hunt and kill other animals for food. They use their sharp teeth to tear meat and their rough tongues to clean off bones.

(right) Lions catch and hold their prey with their sharp teeth.

mane

*(left) Male lions look different from **lionesses**, or females. A male lion grows a long, thick **mane** on his head, neck, and shoulders. Females do not grow manes.*

Leopards (above left) and tigers (above right) are also members of the family Felidae.

Where do lions live?

There are two **species**, or types, of lions: African and Asiatic. Each type is named after the continent where it is found—Africa or Asia. At a glance, it is difficult to tell an Asiatic lion from an African lion.

Asiatic lions have shorter manes than those of African lions, and they have a long fold of skin along their bellies. There are only about 300 wild Asiatic lions left.

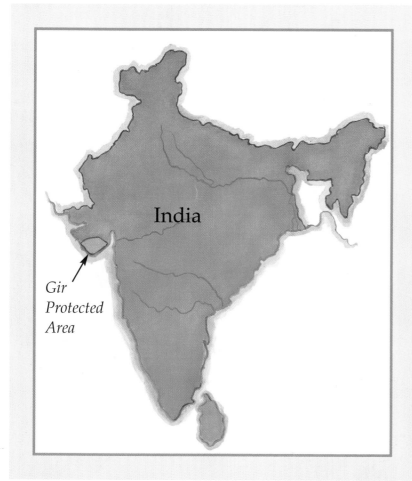

India

Gir Protected Area

Asiatic lions once roamed across southern Europe, the Middle East, and Asia. Today, they are an **endangered** species. The only Asiatic lions still living in the wild are found in a small forest called the Gir Protected Area. It is located in India, a country in Asia.

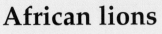

African lions

Most of the world's lions live on the continent of Africa. Between 10,000 and 30,000 African lions live on the **savannah**, or grasslands, of African countries such as Kenya, Uganda, Tanzania, and Botswana. The map on the right shows the African lion's range.

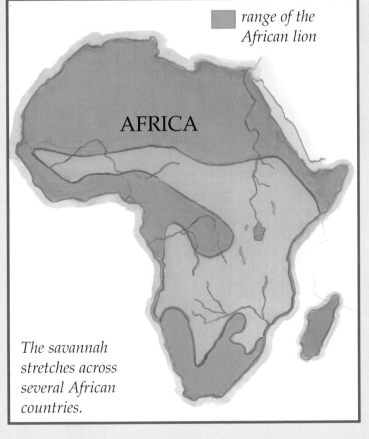

range of the African lion

AFRICA

The savannah stretches across several African countries.

What is a life cycle?

All animals go through a set of changes called a **life cycle**. They are born and then grow and change into adults. As adults, they **reproduce**, or make babies of their own. This book is about the life cycle of an African lion.

A life cycle is not the same as a **life span**. A life span is the length of time an animal lives. In the wild, a lioness might live to be eighteen years old, but her male babies will live to be only about eleven.

The life cycle of a lion

A lion's life cycle begins when a baby lion is born. Lion babies, or **cubs**, are born in **litters** of two or three. They **nurse**, or drink their mother's milk, until they are old enough to eat meat. Cubs continue to grow until they are **mature**, or able to reproduce. Females become mature between two and four years of age. Males are not mature until they are five or six years old. Mature males and females **mate**, or join together to make babies. The females become **pregnant** and give birth. When the cubs are born, a new life cycle begins.

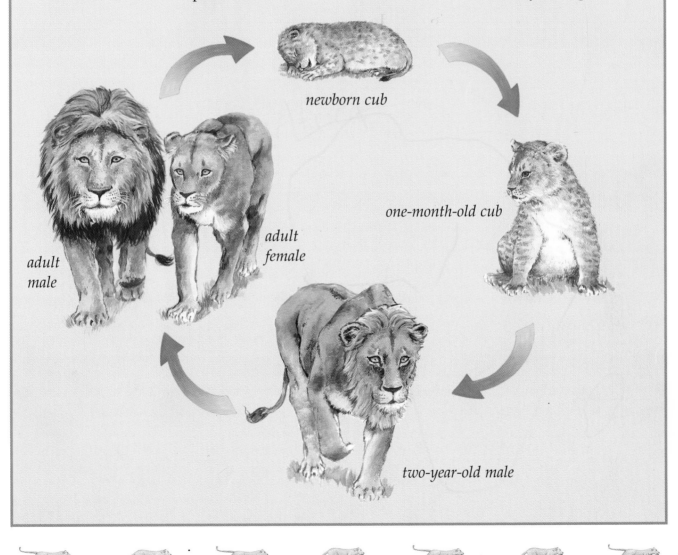

newborn cub

one-month-old cub

adult female

adult male

two-year-old male

 # Life in a pride

Lions are the only cats that live in family groups. A group of lions is called a **pride**. Prides are made up of two to eighteen lionesses and their cubs. Most prides also include up to three adult male lions. Each pride lives in its own area of land, called a **territory**.

In a territory, there is enough **prey** to feed the entire pride. The lions and lionesses hunt prey to feed all the pride members. They also work together to raise and protect their cubs.

These young lions and lionesses belong to a pride.
The lionesses will stay with the pride even as adults.

Dominant males

The adult males of a pride are called **dominant** males because they mate with the females of the pride and keep other males away. They patrol the pride's territory, marking its **boundaries**, or borders, with scent and keeping a keen watch for intruders and prey. Older males must also be on the lookout for young males that may challenge them for their position in the pride.

In areas with good hunting and plenty of fresh water, a pride can grow to a large size.

In the litter

A pregnant lioness carries her cubs inside her body while they **gestate**, or grow and develop. The babies gestate for almost four months. When the lioness is ready to give birth, she moves to a safe, quiet spot away from her pride. The lioness then gives birth to a litter of two, three, or four cubs. Each cub weighs no more than three or four pounds (1.4-1.8 kg) when it is born.

Depending on Mom

The cubs cannot see when they are born. Their mother helps them find her nipples so they can begin to nurse. The cubs keep nursing for about eight months. After six weeks they also start to eat some meat, which their mother brings to them.

*Cubs have spots for **camouflage**. Most spots fade as the cubs grow, but many adult females remain slightly spotted. The spots help hide the females during a hunt.*

In the lion's den

While their mother is hunting, the cubs stay behind in their well-hidden **den**, or shelter. They huddle close to one another and sit very still so that predators will not notice them. Sometimes their mother has to move them. Using her teeth, she picks up the cubs one at a time and carries them to a new hiding place.

Joining the pride

Cubs join the pride when they can move around on their own— usually when they are about two months old. Their mother leads them from their hiding place and introduces them to the other lions and cubs. At first, the cubs are frightened of their big relatives and hide behind their mother.

It does not take long for the cubs to feel comfortable, however. They play with the other cubs and start spending time with the other pride members. Lionesses often "babysit" one another's cubs, as shown above. Cubs even nurse from their babysitter when their mother is away hunting.

Meeting the "mane" guy

The dominant males in the pride are patient with the new members. They allow the cubs to play with their tails. The cubs bat the black tuft at the tip of the tail, just as kittens bat balls of wool. When food is scarce, males are more likely to share a meal with cubs than lionesses are. Sometimes a male even stops the females from feeding so the cubs can eat instead.

Learning the language

Cubs must learn to communicate in order to cooperate with other members of their pride. They hiss, snarl, woof, cough, and growl at one another and at other animals. Each sound has its own meaning. Lions also use **body language** to communicate. They rub their foreheads, faces, or bodies against one another as a greeting.

Growing up

The entire pride cares for the cubs when they are small, but as they grow older, the pride members expect them to do more on their own. The lionesses stop feeding them when they are about ten months old. By then, the cubs must come to a **kill** and learn to compete with one another for their share. They also learn that a kill needs to be defended from hyenas, which often try to steal a meal.

Learning to hunt

Lion cubs love to wrestle and pounce on one another. Playing makes the cubs strong and prepares them for hunting. By the time the cubs are a year old, they start learning how to hunt for themselves. To teach them hunting skills, their mother catches a small animal, such as a hare, and brings it to them alive. The cubs then compete to kill and eat the prey.

 # Ready for life

Female cubs are almost fully grown at a year and a half. They are strong enough to help in hunts, and they begin to **stalk** prey on their own. Female cubs find their place within the pride and stay with their family group for life. As the young males near maturity, however, they are no longer as welcome as when they were cubs.

Time to go!

The male cubs soon have to leave the pride. Only dominant males can mate with pride females, so other males are forced to leave, even before they are fully grown and ready to mate. The young lions leave the pride at around age two, when their manes start to grow. They must try to find a new pride by the time they are fully mature, at about five years. Their departure from their first pride is nature's way of making sure that the young male lions also have a chance to reproduce.

These young males are starting to look like adults. Their bodies are much larger, their manes are beginning to grow in around their necks, and the spots have almost faded from their fur coats.

Adult lions

An adult male can weigh between 385 and 420 pounds (175-190 kg). The appearance of a lion's strong body and heavy mane makes challengers think twice!

A lion's large size is not always helpful, however. It is difficult for a male to sneak up on prey. He is better at hunting large, slow animals.

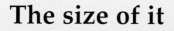

The size of it

Fully grown lionesses weigh between 240 and 285 pounds (110-130 kg). Most are smaller than males. They are also more **agile**, or able to move quickly and suddenly. Lionesses are better suited to hunting small and medium-sized prey. When they crouch down, their fur easily blends in with the savannah to camouflage them.

The tall grass helps hide these lionesses as they lie on the ground.

Dominant males

When they leave their first prides, young male lions often stay together in a group to hunt. After two or three years, they break off into pairs or trios. Brothers usually stay together. They wander and hunt along the boundaries of other pride territories. Soon they will be strong enough to challenge the dominant male or males of one of the prides.

One or two young lions may fight a dominant male or males to take over their roles in a pride. Often, the younger males are strong enough to defeat an older male or males. If the young lions win their challenge, they become the new dominant males of the pride. If they are defeated, they must retreat and continue looking for a pride.

Making babies

Dominant males in a pride mate with each mature female. When a female is ready to mate, she gives off a scent to attract the males.

She produces this scent only when she is in **estrus**, or heat. A lioness goes into estrus when her body is ready to reproduce.

New mates

When new males take over the dominant role in a pride, they have an **instinct** to mate as soon as possible. Part of the reason they join a pride is to mate with females and produce cubs of their own. They are not interested in raising the cubs of other males.

Out of the way

Lionesses that are caring for cubs will not go into estrus, so the new males try to kill all the youngest cubs in the pride. Without cubs, the lionesses naturally go into estrus, and the new dominant males have a better chance of mating with them.

If a lioness does not want to mate, she swats a male with her paw and growls at him.

Top of the food chain

The savannah can be very hot during the day, so lions prefer to hunt at night when it is cool. They are **opportunistic** hunters, however. If they see a chance for a successful hunt during the day, they go for it.

Herds of animals that **graze**, or feed, on the grasslands are the favorite prey of lions. These animals include zebras, buffalo, and wildebeests. Any one of these animals is large enough to feed a pride!

Eating like a lion

In a single day, a lioness can eat up to 55 pounds (25 kg) of meat, and a male lion can devour up to 95 pounds (43 kg)! Lions succeed only three times out of every ten hunts, so they eat as much as they can when food is available. When food is scarce, lions target baby animals or those that are sick or injured because weak animals are easier to catch.

(left) Lions do not always catch their prey. This warthog, for example, got away.

Out of my way!

As soon as lions bring down an animal, the competition for food begins. The dominant males eat first, taking as much as their bellies will hold. Next, the adult females fight for their share. The cubs eat last if they are old enough to feed on their own. When the lions have finished eating, **scavengers** such as this vulture swoop in and eat any leftovers.

Competition for food

Lions, leopards, cheetahs, and hyenas all compete for food. Lions are the only animals that respect pride boundaries, so a pride often finds animals such as hyenas in its territory. When lions find these intruders in their range, they may attack them in order to protect their food supply.

No laughing matter!

Of all the competitors on the plains, hyenas are a pride's worst enemies. Lions and hyenas roam the same land and hunt the same animals. In the past, scientists believed that lions always hunted and hyenas always **scavenged**, or fed on leftovers. They now know that hyenas will fight lions for a fresh kill. A large group of hyenas can chase away a pride and steal its meal. Hyenas will also attack lionesses that are separated from their pride, and they are a serious threat to lion cubs. Lions sometimes attack and kill the dominant females of hyena clans, but they rarely eat them.

Dangers to lions

In spite of their strong bodies and loyal families, lions are in danger. **Poachers**, or people who hunt illegally, kill lions to sell their claws and tails to tourists. Farmers who raise livestock sometimes shoot lions because they attack cattle when they are hungry. The biggest threat to lions, however, is **loss of habitat**.

As people build towns and roads, they use up the land on which lions roam and hunt. Lions that try to stay in their old territories get shot, especially if they attack people or farm animals. The remaining lions are pushed into smaller areas. As a result, they have less food, water, and space in which to move around.

Deadly diseases

In Africa, lion populations are still fairly strong. Diseases can kill lions, but the prides live far enough apart that illnesses do not spread easily.

Disease is a much bigger threat in Asia, where the few lions that are left live close together. Scientists fear that all the lions living within the limits of the Gir Protected Area could die if a serious disease broke out.

Helping lions

Many people in the world want to help lions. The government of India and those of many African countries have set aside protected areas for lions and other wildlife. In these areas, it is against the law to kill lions.

Scientists also hope to introduce lions to other areas, especially in Asia. They believe that the number of Asiatic lions could grow if some lions were moved to other parts of the continent.

Get involved!

Even though lions may live far away from you, there are ways that you can help them. The best way to help lions is to learn about them and their problems. Read about the work scientists are doing. If you decide their research is helpful, you can support them by helping to raise money for their work.

There are several great websites about lions and the people working to help them. For information on Asiatic lions, visit www.asiatic-lion.org. If you would like to learn more about African lions and other African wildlife, go to www.awf.org. At www.lioncentral.org and www.lionresearch.org, you can learn about lions everywhere.

The legend of Androcles and the Lion

During the time when gladiators fought lions in the Roman Coliseum, there lived a slave named Androcles. One night, Androcles ran away from his master and hid in a forest, where he encountered a lion in great pain. The lion had a thorn in its paw. Androcles was brave enough to take the lion's paw in his hands and remove the thorn. Later, when Androcles was caught and forced to become a gladiator, he met the lion again—in the ring! The lion recognized Androcles and would not fight him. It is said that Androcles and the lion were friendly companions from that day on. You never know when you might need a lion's help. It pays to help lions!

Glossary

Note: Boldfaced words defined in the book may not appear in the glossary.

body language A way of sending messages by using posture, gestures, and facial expressions

camouflage Skin colors and patterns that help plants and animals blend in with their surroundings

endangered Describing a plant or animal species in danger of disappearing from the Earth

instinct An animal's natural knowledge or desire

kill A dead animal that is eaten by other animals

litter A group of baby animals born to one mother at the same time

loss of habitat The reduction of natural places where plants and animals live

pregnant Describing a female carrying one or more unborn babies inside her body

prey An animal that is hunted and eaten by other animals

scavenger An animal that feeds on leftover meat instead of hunting

stalk To track and sneak up on prey while hunting

territory An area of land claimed and defended by a pride

Index

1 2 3 4 5 6 7 8 9 0   Printed in the U.S.A.   1 0 9 8 7 6 5 4 3 2